DATE DUE			
JUL 5 '00			
JUL 18 '00			
AUG 28 00			
JAN 5 '01			
JUL 16 '02			
AUG 1 2 2002			
AUG 20 '02			
OCT 2 1 20			

5/00

JACKSON COUNTY
Library Services

HEADQUARTERS
413 West Main Street
Medford, Oregon 97501

GIANT OCTOPUSES

by Christine Zuchora-Walske

photographs by Fred Bavendam

Pull Ahead Books

⌐ Lerner Publications Company • Minneapolis

Website address: www.lernerbooks.com

Lerner Publications Company
A Division of Lerner Publishing Group
241 First Avenue North
Minneapolis, MN 55401 U.S.A.

Words in *italic type* are explained in a glossary
on page 30.

Library of Congress Cataloging-in-Publication Data

Zuchora-Walske, Christine.
    Giant octopuses / by Christine Zuchora-Walske ;
  photographs by Fred Bavendam.
       p.   cm. — (Pull ahead books)
    Includes index.
    Summary: Introduces the physical characteristics,
  behavior, and habitat of the giant octopus.
    ISBN 0-8225-3633-1 (hardcover : alk. paper). —
    ISBN 0-8225-3637-4 (paperback : alk. paper)
    1. Octopus—Juvenile literature.
  [1. Octopus.] I. Bavendam, Fred, ill. II. Title.
  III. Series.
  QL430.3.02Z835 2000
  594'.56—dc21   99–24721

Manufactured in the United States of America
1 2 3 4 5 6 – JR – 05 04 03 02 01 00

What is hiding in the small space between these rocks?

This animal is a giant octopus.
It lives in the sea.

A giant octopus can be bigger
than a grown-up person.

How can such a big animal
fit into a small space?

An octopus has a soft body
with no bones.

A soft body can fit into a space
of any shape.

A soft body
can also
squeeze
through a
very small
hole!

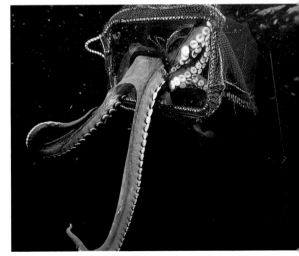

An octopus has many arms
that bend easily.

How many arms can you
count on this octopus?

All eight arms have round
cups called *suckers* on them.

Suckers help an octopus taste,
smell, feel, and hold onto things.

An octopus's arms stick out from its body.

The layer of skin covering an octopus's body is called its *mantle.*

Many important body parts
are on or under the mantle.

What body part is watching you
in this picture?

A tube called a *funnel*
sticks out of the mantle.

The funnel of
this octopus
is right under
one eye.

To swim, an octopus squirts
water from its funnel.

Each squirt pushes the octopus
through the water.

An octopus can also squirt
dark ink from its funnel.

The ink smells like an octopus.

It helps the octopus trick
predators and get away.

Predators are animals that
hunt and eat other animals.

Octopuses are predators, too.

This octopus is stretching up,
looking for an animal to eat.

Look! Now it is walking
across the seafloor.

Surprise! The octopus quickly jumps on two crabs.

How will it eat the crabs?

First it will rip up the crabs
with its arms.

Then it will eat the crabs
with its hard, sharp *beak.*

The beak is under the mantle,
at the center of the arms.

What other animals have beaks?

Like birds, octopuses have babies that come from eggs.

A mother octopus hangs many, many eggs inside her *den.*

A den is a cozy, safe place to live.

The mother watches over her
eggs. She never leaves them.

She squirts water on them
and brushes dirt off them.

After many weeks, baby
octopuses *hatch* from the eggs.

A newborn giant octopus is
as big as your smallest fingernail.

Many baby octopuses are
eaten by predators.

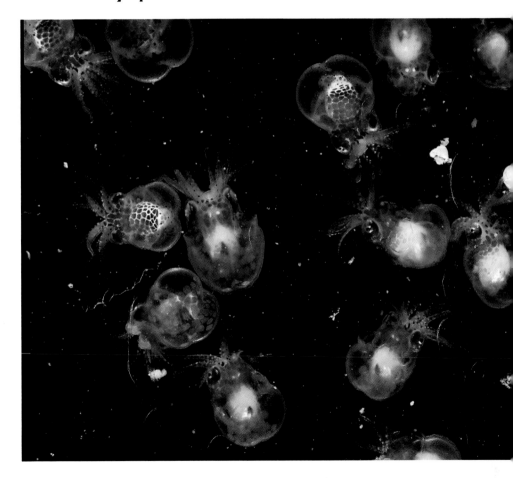

A few babies stay safe and find plenty to eat. They grow up fast.

Soon they are fully grown.

They walk, swim, hunt,
and hide in the sea.

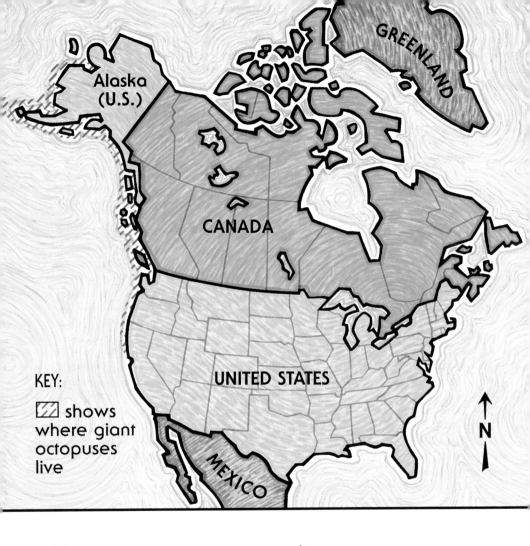

KEY:

🔲 shows
where giant
octopuses
live

Alaska
(U.S.)

CANADA

GREENLAND

UNITED STATES

N

MEXICO

Find your state or province on this map.
Do octopuses live near you?

Parts of a Giant Octopus's Body

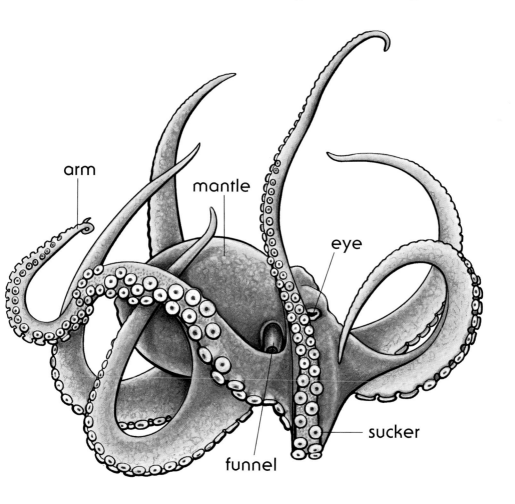

arm

mantle

eye

funnel

sucker

Glossary

beak: a hard mouth with sharp edges

den: a cozy, safe place to live

funnel: a tube that sticks out of an octopus's mantle. An octopus can squirt water or ink from its funnel.

hatch: come out

mantle: the layer of skin covering most of an octopus's body.

predators: animals that hunt and eat other animals

suckers: round cups on octopus arms. Suckers help an octopus taste, smell, feel, and hold onto things.

Hunt and Find

- **baby octopuses** on pages 24–25
- octopuses **eating** on pages 19–20, 26
- octopus **eggs** on pages 21–24
- an octopus **hiding** on page 3
- an octopus **squirting ink** on pages 14–15
- octopuses **stretching up** on pages 12, 16

The publisher wishes to extend special thanks to our **series consultant,** Sharyn Fenwick. An elementary science-math specialist, Mrs. Fenwick was the recipient of the National Science Teachers Association 1991 Distinguished Teaching Award. In 1992, representing the state of Minnesota at the elementary level, she received the Presidential Award for Excellence in Math and Science Teaching.

Edward Clark

About the Author

Christine Zuchora-Walske grew up in Minnesota. Later, she lived near Chicago for several years. She often visited Chicago's John G. Shedd Aquarium, and there she fell in love with all kinds of water animals. Christine enjoys doing anything outdoors— especially swimming. She also likes to read, make music, and write and edit books for children. She wrote *Peeking Prairie Dogs* and *Leaping Grasshoppers* for Lerner's Pull Ahead series. Christine now lives in Minneapolis with her husband, Ron.

About the Photographer

Fred Bavendam is an American photographer who specializes in marine and natural history topics. His stories have been published in many magazines, including *National Geographic* and *International Wildlife*. Bavendam attended the University of New Hampshire and graduated with majors in art and zoology. He resides in New Hampshire and spends most of the year diving in remote locations around the world.